THE ADVENTURES

OF DUC

OF NOYO HARBOR

California Sea Lion Story

Based on actual events

By brad caylor

DEDICATION

This story is dedicated to all of the Marine Mammal Rescue Centers and volunteers that help protect our marine resources.

ACKNOWLEDGMENTS

Special thanks to John and Brandon at The Noyo Fishing Center for their story input that got me started on this project in the first place.

Thanks to my wife Sondra for the image of Duc. It fits his character perfect. Maybe some day Duc's image will represent the fight against ocean trash.

And thanks to my granddaughter Cheyanne for helping Sondra with the illustrations throughout the story.

Thanks to Ed More of "Wildlifeworkshop.com" for the use of their reproductions of the Wolf eels, crabs, abalone and scallops.

Thanks to all those at The Marine Rescue Center for all the information on Duc and other marine mammals that have come through the rescue center.

Thanks to Sue Smith for editing this story while on vacation, sitting by the camp fire at MacKerricher State Park. Thank you.

And a special thanks to Oprah. Just in case she reads this heart warming story and recommends it to her friends.

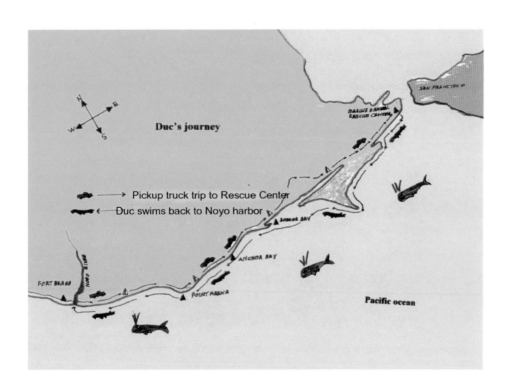

Follow Duc's trip back home on any California map.

The Adventures of Duc

One bright sunny morning after John, the owner of the Noyo Fishing Center, opened up the store, he walked across the road to the boat docks on the Noyo River to check on his rental kayaks. He wanted to make sure the old sea lion's that slept on the docks hadn't pushed his kayaks off into the river like they had once before.

All the kayaks were still on the dock but there was something else laying there that caught his eye. There was a very young sea lion lying on the dock with that please-help-me look in his eyes. This little sea lion was covered with fishing line that someone had carelessly left in the water and it was wrapped all around his neck and front flippers. John knew that if he did not get that fishing line off of this young pup he would probably drown.

John ran back across the road to the fishing center and got some small herring fish that he kept in the freezer for people to use for bait when fishing in the ocean. He grabbed a pair of scissors and then out the door and back over to the docks. John had to be very careful not to scare the young sea lion so he sat down as close as he could and then coaxed him closer with the treat. The young sea lion seemed to know that John was there to help him and watched closely with his big brown eyes as John reached around his neck and cut the fishing line from his neck and flippers. " There," John said, "you stay out of trouble."

The young sea lion moved off of the dock into the water and thanked John with a couple of barks and a big smile. This was the beginning of a lasting friendship.

      For the next few weeks the young pup just
spent his time learning how to be a resident sea lion,
never getting too far from the fish market, playing with the
other sea lions and harbor seals, floating on his back in
the sun, swimming up and down the river alongside the
fishing boats as they entered and left the harbor.
Sometimes he would swim out in front of the restaurants
overlooking the river and show off to the kids looking out
the windows and then head back up the river to the fish

market to look for Brandon who cleaned fish for the market. If he played his cards right he would always get there just when Brandon threw the fresh scraps into the water and he would be there to gobble them up.

The fish market is built out over the river bank and on high tide the water comes close to the bottom of the concrete floor in one of the cleaning areas. There is an 8 inch diameter hole in the floor that's used as a drain for this part of the market. This little guy knows about this hole. So when there is a high tide and he knows Brandon is there, he sticks his head up through the hole and barks for his treat from Brandon.

It had been two weeks since his encounter with the fishing line and the injuries to his neck had healed. He was back to his old self again, headed for trouble.

One day while doing his acrobatics and underwater maneuvers to impress his friends, he encountered a piece of gray duct tape floating in the river that someone had carelessly thrown into the water. It was about twenty feet long and two inches wide. He grabbed the tape at one end with his sharp little teeth and started swimming up and down the river, twisting around and around, showing off, and not paying any attention to what the tape was doing. Pretty soon the tape was wrapped around his whole body and his flippers were taped to his sides. Now he was in serious trouble because he almost could not move in the water.

Lucky for him, the young sea lion just happened to be right next to the boat dock where his new friend had saved him before when he got tangled up in old fishing line. He worked his way over to the dock by wiggling his tail back and forth. But it was late and getting dark and everyone had gone home. Now he was getting scared, the tape was getting tighter, choking him and he could barley move. The young pup knew he had to do something quick or he would sink to the bottom of the river and nobody would ever know what happened to him. All the grownup sea lions and harbor seals had gone down the river to the ocean for dinner. They would probably spend the night on the beach, too far away from the dock to hear his cries for help. He put his chin up on the boat dock and just kept wiggling his back flippers until he worked his way up onto the dock. It was very dark now and he was alone and scared. The young sea lion barked a few times but no one came. He was exhausted now so he laid his head down and fell asleep.

THE YOUNG SEA LION ASLEEP ON THE DOCK

Early the next morning, as the warm sun came into the harbor, the young sea lion was awakened when he heard his friends talking in the distance. By now the pup was so weak he could barley lift his head.   He laid there and barked as loud as he could to get their attention. John and Brandon ran over to the boat dock where they could see the young sea lion was in trouble again.

After looking at all of the tape wrapped around the sea lion, they felt it would be too dangerous to try and remove it by themselves. They might get bitten or maybe even hurt the sea lion.

John got out his cell phone and called the Fish and Game Department, who have an office right at the harbor, and told them about the sea lion in distress. The Fish and Game office called the Marine Mammal Rescue Center at Fort Cronkite in Sausalito, California about 160 miles south of Noyo Harbor, and told them about the young sea lion. The people at the Rescue Center help hundreds of marine mammals and birds every year and know what to do in an emergency. The Rescue Center alerted their volunteers in Fort Bragg to check on the injured sea lion and see how they could help.

When they saw the trouble the pup was in they wasted no time. They unloaded a large animal cage out of the pickup truck and took it down onto the dock being very careful not to scare the little guy. They talked to him for a while and then coaxed him into the cage with a fresh fish treat and a little help from one of the volunteers. The young sea lion really didn't need too much coaxing because by now he was very tired and hungry and he just knew these people were here to help him.

John and Brandon and the two Mammal Center volunteers carried the cage up the dock ramp and loaded it into the pickup truck. Checking the sea lion to make sure he was comfortable and safe, they headed up to the highway to start their 160 mile journey south on the Mendocino Coast Highway towards the Rescue Center.

On his way to the Rescue Center

After driving one and half hours, and fifty-five

miles, the volunteers came to the little coastal town of Anchor Bay. There they met up with two more volunteers that drove up from the Rescue Center to pick up the sea lion, give him some nourishment, and continue the trip south one hundred and fifteen miles and three hours on the road. Soon the young sea lion was fast asleep.

When they finally reached the Rescue Center the tired young sea lion was quickly taken to the animal hospital where workers wet him down, gave him antibiotics, and very carefully removed all the tape. He knew he was in good hands because everyone had smiles on their faces and treated him very nice. He was checked out and found to have no serious injuries but was a little under nourished from the long truck ride and being wrapped up in duct tape for two days. The pup was given a nice warm bath, dinner of fresh herring, and put to bed in his own condo.

By now the staff members had given the young sea lion a new name, Duc, short for duct tape, and an orange tag clipped to his flipper labeling him patient No. 25016. Duc slept like a baby all night, because after all, he was still just a baby.

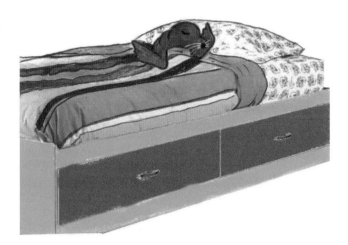

Duc is sleeping in his new bed at the Rescue Center, dreaming of his friends back in the Noyo River.

Duc's first day at the Rescue Center was spent laying around his condo area, he swam in the pool and got to know his neighbors, other sea lions, like Rumpers, a sea lion that was entangled in fishing nets discarded in the ocean by someone that does not realize how these nets can harm marine life. Inuyasha, another young sea lion that was caught in fish netting and it got tightly wrapped around her neck and cut into her throat. She almost starved to death. Then there were Tarhead, Cha Cha and Scooter, just to name a few. The shelter was filled with many more sea lions, harbor seals, pelicans, sea birds, otters and other marine mammals, all nursing one kind of injury or another caused by people discarding their trash in the ocean, mostly from plastic debris. Duc was thinking that this was a pretty good deal. Three meals a day and all the love and affection he could stand from his captors.

This was a pretty good deal for Duc

Yes, this was real nice, but he was thinking about his friends at Noyo Harbor, the small harbor seals, the huge older sea lions that he would torment by chasing around them, and the old pelican he would scare by coming right up underneath him in the river. He missed those choice pieces of fish that Brandon would throw to him from the fish cleaning table, and all the grownups and kids that would wave to him as he swam up and down the river. Yes, this was nice, but he wanted to go home, home to his friends in the Noyo River.

The next morning Duc heard the Doctor saying that he thought Duc would be ready for his trip back home. This was the news Duc had been waiting to hear. After breakfast and a nice dip in the pool, the volunteers loaded Duc into a cage and up into the bed of the pickup truck. They drove down the road away from the Rescue Center and headed north. Duc couldn't believe it, they were going to give him a ride all the way back home to the Noyo harbor, or so he thought.

After driving about ten minutes the truck turned left onto an old bumpy road to the ocean. The driver stopped the truck and Duc could hear the waves crashing on the beach. The driver and helper opened the tail gate and carried the cage and Duc down to the waters edge. Then she opened the cage door and said, "okay Duc, time to go home."

Duc looked around, all he could see was ocean, lots of it. He scooted out into the water a few feet and turned around to see if the volunteers were just joking and would load him back up and take him home. No such luck. He swam out into the ocean about fifty feet and turned around just in time to see people taking pictures, waving good by and saying "good luck Duc, be careful out there and stay out of trouble.

Duc's friends waving goodby.

This wasn't like the Noyo River he lived in where he could see both sides and had many friends around him. This was the ocean, and it was huge, and cold, with big waves and no telling what was out there. Duc swam out from the beach to get away from the pounding waves. He had no idea which way to go and this thought was very scary for him. He knew he was way too small and too young to be alone in this huge, cold, scary ocean, and that the rescue people should have taken him all the way home and put him back into friendly waters, like in the Noyo river where he came from.

Duc looks very small in this big ocean

Duc swam out to some rocks sticking up out of the water where he came face to face with a giant sea turtle, something that he had never seen before. It seemed that the sea turtle was just like Duc. He had just been released from the rescue center and was sitting on the rocks wondering which way to go. Duc couldn't quite figure out this new discovery. All the Giant turtle had to do was stick his legs and head out of his house and swim, pretty neat.

Duc was scared at first by the size of this guy, but then he noticed an orange tag clipped to the turtle's shell. The big turtle told Duc how he was saved by the rescue center when he had plastic string wrapped around his neck and couldn't eat. "A fisherman saw me on a beach somewhere and thought I looked pretty bad so he called the Rescue Center and their volunteers came and got me and took me to their hospital and fixed me up".

Duc and the Sea turtle talked for a while about their friends at the Rescue Center. Duc told the turtle that he was from the Noyo river, that he had to get back home as soon as possible. The turtle said, "Head north, it is a long way up there and be very careful because there are a lot of mean characters in the ocean between here and the Noyo River". The sea turtle said he would send word to the big Grey whales that are headed north, and all the sea lion colonies along the coast to watch out for a very small sea lion headed up the coast to the Noyo River and to help him get home safely. Duc didn't know what the Sea turtle meant by "mean characters," but he thanked him and took off like a rocket headed north, headed home.

DUC LISTENS TO INSTRUCTIONS FROM THE
GIANT TURTLE

DUC STARTS HIS LONG JOURNEY HOME

A full grown California sea lion can swim up to twenty-four mile per hour. Duc wasn't full grown. He was only about four months old and very small, about forty pounds, but he could glide through the water pretty fast. Like any youngster, he was curious about everything around him and that slowed him down a little.

After swimming at top speed for a while Duc came up to the surface for some air and to take a look around. He could feel there was something close to him. Duc looked back and could see three huge sharks. Duc had heard about Great White sharks at the Rescue Center and how they would eat sea lions. The sharks were looking right at the young sea lion. All Duc could see was teeth, lots of teeth, and very mean eyes. Duc got very scared and quickly dove down into the thick kelp that covered the ocean floor. The ocean kelp is like an underwater forest and a good place for this little sea lion to hide. Duc kept swimming north weaving in and out of the kelp so the sharks could not see him. After a very long exhausting swim Duc thought it would be safe to come up for some air and take a look around. But when he stuck his head out of the water the sharks came out of nowhere and were right on his tail again. Now there were four hungry sharks looking for lunch. Duc figured his only chance to get away from the sharks was to try to get to shore. He would have to swim faster than he ever had if he wanted to stay alive.

The sharks were getting closer and closer. Duc spotted a small island out in front of him, just big enough to get him out of the water. If he could get there before the sharks got to him he would be safe, safe for now. The biggest shark was only about five feet from Duc's rear flipper with his mouth open wide. Duc looked back and all he could see was lots of big sharp teeth getting ready to chomp down on his flippers. He dove down and then came up as fast as he could and flew right out of the water and onto the small rocky island. The sharks stopped at the waters edge only inches away from Duc. A close call, Duc was very scared and shaken and had a few sore spots from landing on the rocky island, but he wasn't going to be lunch for a bunch of ugly sharks.

DUC ALMOST LOST A FLIPPER

It was getting late and Duc didn't think it would be a good idea to get back into the ocean in the dark, so he decided to spend the night on the rocks. Now he knew what the giant sea turtle meant when he said there were mean characters out here. Duc stretched out on a small flat spot on the rocks and was soon fast asleep, dreaming of his friends back home.

The next morning the sun was warm and the ocean was flat, like the river where he lived. Duc looked around and couldn't see any signs of sharks in the area. He could see water spouts way out in the distance. He knew that the big grey whales were keeping and eye on him. This made Duc feel a little safer. He dove into the ocean and headed north grabbing a little snack of herring and sardines here and there along the way.

Duc saw a school of dolphins swimming north and he noticed how fast they could swim. They would swim under water then leap out into the air then back under water. He was going to have to try this. While he watched the dolphins, Duc swam right into a large pile of ocean trash that was floating on the surface of the water. It was like a raft of plastic bottles, string, bags and small bits of plastic and fishing line. Everything all stuck together. Duc saw something yellow in the middle of the pile and his curiosity got the best of him. He had to investigate. He closed his mouth and dove under the trash pile and came up with a pair of yellow diving goggles hanging on his head. He remembered someone at the Rescue Center wearing something like this while they were cleaning the pools. They made everything look very bright and he could see a lot further under water, so he just kept them on. Now he could swim almost as fast as the dolphins and not get any trash in his eyes.

DUC'S NEW GOGGLES

Duc tried swimming with the dolphins for a while but they were just too fast. The dolphins swam out of site and Duc was left swimming all alone again.

It seemed like everywhere Duc looked there was some new kind of creature swimming by him or crawling on the ocean floor or even sticking their heads out of the rocks. When he saw a small fishing boat anchored in front of him with an air hose going down into the water, he had to investigate. A man on the boat was watching Duc because the sea lion was getting close to the air hose.

Being the curious young sea lion that he was, he followed the air hose down deep into the water where he found an urchin diver wearing a black rubber suit and breathing through an air hose. The diver was taking sea urchins off of the rocks and putting them into a wire basket that was tied to a rope. When the basket was full, the man on the boat would pull it up and empty the urchins into the boat and then send the basket back down to the diver to fill it up again. This was all very interesting to watch, but time was wasting and Duc had to get home.

Duc watching the Urchin diver

Cruising along, swimming just fast enough to make good time but not get too tired, he saw a large school of herring right in his path. Duc figured this would be a good time to have a snack. So he swam through the school with his mouth wide open and that did the trick. Now Duc had a full stomach.

It was a beautiful sunny day. Duc got a little sleepy after his snack, so he figured maybe he could just float on his back for a while and soak up a little sun while he took a nap.

"WAKE UP, WAKE UP". Duc could hardly believe what he was

hearing. But here was a baby grey whale that was traveling with her mother to Alaska, yelling at him, "get going, there are killer whales in the area and they love to eat baby sea lions". She didn't have to tell Duc twice. He thanked her for the warning and took off, watching for the killer whales and looking for places to hide just in case.

Duc swam fast and straight until almost dark when he heard the sounds of breakers hitting a beach and the sounds of sea lion's. Swimming to where a big river emptied into the ocean he found a colony of sea lions and seals lying on the beach. The biggest sea lion he had ever seen came down to the waters edge to greet Duc. "We heard that a young sea lion was traveling north alone. You can spend the night here with us where you will be safe", said the old sea lion. Then the old sea lion waddled back up the beach and lay down with his friends. This was good news to Duc because he had traveled a long way today and he could use a good nights sleep.

The beach had piles of old kelp that had washed up with all kinds of trash mixed in it, plastic bottles, rope, fishing line and old netting making it hard to find a clean place to sleep. Duc wondered how many other marine mammals would end up at the rescue center with all this trash in the water and on the beach. He found a spot of clean sand, made a small hole for his body with his flippers and settled into the warm sand for the night. Thinking of his friends back home, he was soon fast asleep.

The next morning the whole colony woke up and headed out into the ocean for breakfast. Duc told his story, to a few that would listen, about how he ended up at the rescue center and all the new friends he had met. He was reminded again by the old sea lion about the dangers lurking in the ocean and to be very careful. Duc thanked everyone for letting him stay on the beach with them for the night. Duc checked the ocean further out just to make sure the big grey whales were still keeping an eye on him. He spotted the spouts, time to go. He was headed north, headed home.

So far the trip had been fairly safe except for those mean old sharks, but they were no match for this feisty young sea lion, a sea lion on a mission. If he could just keep up the speed and stay out of trouble he would be back in the Noyo Harbor in a day and a half. But just as soon as he got into cruise mode, it got very dark in the water. Looking up towards the surface Duc could see the white bellies of three huge killer whales swimming right over him. Duc slowed down and dove deeper into the kelp, always keeping and eye on the killer whales above him. It seemed like they were looking for him but they couldn't see him in the kelp. Duc had to come up with a plan because he was going to run out of air very soon. He thought, if he came up to the surface and got his air behind them, they would think he turned around and was going south. This way he could go back down to the kelp and head north just as fast as he could. This was a good plan, but it didn't work. When Duc came up for air, one of the whales spotted him and started chasing him. The killer whale was a lot faster than Duc had thought. The whale grabbed Duc by the rear flipper and threw him into the air. Duc landed next to another killer whale and started swimming as fast as he could to get away.

Scared to death that the whales where going to eat him, Duc swam to a passing fishing trawler, he swam under the boat and came up on the other side where the whales couldn't see him. The whales swam along one side of trawler with Duc swimming along the other side. Pretty soon the whales gave up the search for the little sea lion, not knowing he was just on the other side of the boat. Duc had a few scratches and teeth marks in his flippers.

For a young sea lion that had never been in the ocean before, he was doing pretty good, fooling both the sharks and the Killer whales. But Duc wasn't home yet, so he swam along side the trawler for a while just in case.   Swimming next to the trawler was a good idea. The deck hand on board saw the young sea lion swimming along side the boat and threw him some fresh fish that he had been cleaning on board. This reminded Duc of Brandon at the fish market. He had to get home.

KILLER WHALES LOOKING FOR DUC

Duc dove down deep swimming over a sandy bottom, and sometimes there were rocky areas, where he saw lots of creatures that he had never seen before, like abalone, scallops and big crabs.   With his new goggles he could really see well.

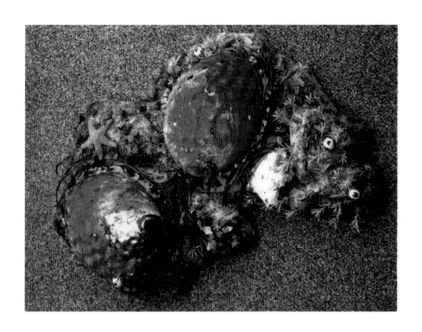

DUC COULD SEE ABALONE AND STAR FISH ON THE ROCKY
OCEAN FLOOR .

BIG CRABS AND SCALLOPS LIKE TO HIDE IN THE ROCKS
WHERE THEY ARE PROTECTED FROM PREDETORS .

Duc swam down close to the rocks to get a better look at the sea
creatures when something caught his eye that really scared him.

Sticking their heads out of a hole in the rocks were two wolf eels, probably the ugliest things he had ever seen. One of the eel's had a crab leg sticking out of its mouth. They were about five feet long and looking right at him. Duc thought that maybe he should stay away from these mean looking guys and just keep going.

WOLF EELS

Sometimes Duc would see other sea lions chasing schools of

salmon or small fish, like herring and anchovies. Full grown sea lions can eat up to thirty pounds of fish a day.

Duc even saw one older sea lion with an orange tag on his flipper and scars around his neck. Probably another victim of some kind of ocean trash or old fishing netting left behind. Whatever it was, he looked fine now. Duc wanted to join them but he knew that his friends in Noyo Harbor were worried about him. He had to get home.

Swimming on the surface for a while so he could see the Mendocino Coast, he saw the bow of a large fishing trawler coming right at him. He had no time to even think about it. He dove down deep and fast just in time, as the propellers of the boat passed over him, missing him by only inches. That was a close call, Duc thought. That Skipper should be more careful, there's a pretty important sea lion out here trying to get home.

After the trawler had passed, he stuck his head up out of the water and saw "Salmon Getter" on the back of the boat. He had seen that boat before, docked in the Noyo Harbor.

Duc was getting excited now, he had to be getting close, and he could taste the river water. He knew he was getting close to home.

ANOTHER CLOSE CALL

Soon after the near miss by the boats propellers, Duc got back into cruise mode when the baby grey whale swam up next to him. She said her mom thought that was a great move he had put on the killer whales earlier in the day, but to be very careful because they were still out there and they could sneak up on you when you let your guard down, and to watch out for fishing boats because we are getting close to Noyo Harbor. There will be many more fishing boats in the area with very dangerous propellers that can cut you in half if they hit you. Tell me about it, Duc thought. "And by the way", she said, "You look pretty cool with those goggles."

The young whale left Duc and headed back out to her mother and the rest of the pod of whales that were all headed north to their feeding grounds up in Alaska.

Duc was getting tired from a very full day of travel, being chased by killer whales, almost hit by a fishing trawler and chasing down food. He thought he would call it a day and look for a good place to sleep for the night.

A rock cropping next to a beach covered with a colony of sea lions looked like a safe place to spend his last night on the ocean. Duc swam over to the area where all the sea lions were sleeping. He found a nice flat spot where he would be safe and laid down. Soon it was dark.

Looking up at the stars he wondered what tomorrow would be like when he made his grand entrance into the Noyo River.

Duc woke up very early the next morning to the sounds of waves crashing on the beach. "This is going to be a beautiful day he thought to himself," He slid off the rocks and swam over to a tide pool and checked himself his reflection in the water. He looked good. He was ready for the final day of his journey. He said goodbye to his friends on the rocks and swam out into the deep water.

Duc checked the ocean to see if the grey whales were still with him, yep, still there, time to go.

There were many fishing boats in the area now, familiar ones he had swam up and down the river with. He recognized voices coming from one of the trawlers, "SEAL THE DEAL" out of Noyo Harbor. This boat had a platform on the back for dragging in their huge fishing nets, and was heading north.

Duc had hitched rides on this platform before, just for the fun of it, when the boat was coming up the river from a fishing trip. But the river was smooth with no big waves and the boats go a lot slower in the river. This was going to be a little tricky. He built up speed flying from wave to wave just like the porpoises had taught him. He knew he could do it. After all , he made a great jump out of the water when the Great White Sharks were after him. When he got close to the platform he gave an extra boost of power and flew right out of the water and up onto the platform.

This went a lot better than he thought it would and the guys on the boat gave him a big hand and were cheering when he made the jump. Now all he had to do was sit back and enjoy the ride.

DUC ON THE PLATFORM WITH A FREE RIDE

After riding on the platform for a while, Duc peeked around the back of the boat and he could see, way off in the distance, the big red buoy that marked the channel to the harbor entrance. Duc had heard stories about how the big old sea lion's would climb up onto the buoy and bark at the fishing boats as they came by. Duc wasn't old enough or big enough to get up onto the buoy yet, but someday he would be there with the rest of them, barking and smiling for the tourist taking pictures.

A FAMILIAR SCENE UP AND DOWN THE COAST

Anywhere there is a harbor, you will find buoys right out side the harbor in the ocean that guide the boats into the rivers safely. Sea lions jump once up out of the water and onto the plat form. Sea lions are very sociable mammals. What do you think they are talking about.

It was time for the trawler to turn right, pass by two more buoys and head into the river. This is where Duc got off. He could ride all the way into the harbor, but there were big waves and Duc had a better idea.

He swam out to the grey whales and thanked them for watching over him and keeping him company on his long journey home and said goodbye.

When he turned around to head into the river he could see all the old sea lions on the buoy watching him. There were lots of people up on the Noyo Bridge and along the bluffs with their cameras waiting for Duc to make his move.   If he could catch a wave, a big wave, he could surf all the way to the river and everyone would know just how cool he was. Duc watched and waited for the biggest wave and swam up to the crest. He did it! He was on his way, surfing like a pro.

Duc surfed by another red buoy, then a green buoy, toward the bridge. Only about two hundred feet to go as the wave was roaring towards the rock wall at the entrance to the river. He leaned over on his side and waved his flipper with the orange tag at the Pomo Indian children standing on the bluffs. They all waved back and cheered him on. Then he leaned over on his other side and waved to all the people standing on the bluffs at the Pomo State Park and on the balconies at the motel next to the bridge. Then the wave got very quiet and set Duc down right at the entrance of the river.

DUC CATCHING THE BIGGEST WAVE

All the sea lions, harbor seals, otters, and even the old pelicans took notice of their young sea lion friend swimming up the middle of the river, past the restaurants, and fishing boats at the docks along the river. Duc rolled over and did the back stroke just so everyone could see his orange tag. To Duc, this was more like a badge of honor. As he made the sweeping left-hand turn in the river and headed for his old dock, he could see Brandon at the fish cleaning market, cleaning fish. Duc heard him yell "Hey John, Troubles back," and he threw Duc a choice piece of fish. "Welcome back buddy," John yelled back, "He's not tangled up in anything is he".

Duc made a few quick dives and came up under his old sea lion friend just to let him know that the troublesome little sea lion was back. Then he dove down and came up under the pelican, scaring him half to death. It was great to be home.

DUC SCARING THE OLD PELICAN

Duc had traveled about one hundred and sixty miles to the Rescue center by road, spent about two days at the center, swam about one hundred and forty miles back home, and was only gone from the harbor for five days. He had a few close encounters with some real mean characters, great white sharks, killer whales, two wolf eels and almost got ran over by several fishing boats. But he made a lot of new friends along the way and found out that he could do anything he put his mind to. This is a pretty impressive story for a six month old sea lion no bigger than your average four year old child.

Duc had never been out of the harbor or away from home until his encounter with the duct tape. He is now a seasoned traveler and still lives in the Noyo harbor in Fort Bragg, California and still wears his badge proudly. Duc has lots of stories to tell his friends.

DUC SHOWING OFF HIS NEW BADGE

DUC TELLING HIS FRIENDS ABOUT HIS JOURNEY

THE WOLF EELS

The wolf eel is not as mean as Duc thought they were. In fact they are very friendly to divers. They can grow to about eight feet long. Their favorite foods are sea urchins, crabs and scallops.

SEA URCHIN

This is what the diver was taking off the rock on the sea bottom when Duc stopped to watch. Sea urchins are harvested for their eggs, that orange yellow area inside the urchin. The urchin is spit open and the eggs are removed and washed several times, then shipped all over the world, because some cultures eat them raw. Wolf eels eat the whole thing. When you visit the ocean, look in the tide pools. That's where you can find them.

THE NOYO FISHING CENTER AT NOYO HARBOR, FORT BRAGG CA.

This is where I live and where my journey began.

That's it, my whole story up til now. I hope you have learned a little about life in the ocean, the problems caused by ocean trash and what I encountered on my journey back home. Come down to the harbor and visit me and my friends when your in town.

A WORD FROM DUC ON

OCEAN TRASH

I was very lucky when I got wrapped up in the duct tape and fishing line floating in the Noyo River because there was someone there to help me. When a marine mammal gets into discarded trash in the Ocean there is no one to help, and they are often injured very badly.

This is Rumpers and Inuyash who were both saved just in time by The Rescue Center. Each year more than 100,000 marine mammals, sea turtles and sea birds are killed by becoming entangled or digesting ocean trash. You can learn more about the rescue center's, watch videos and meet more marine mammals that have been saved by the rescue centers and their volunteers. Just go on the internet and type in, MarineMammalRescuecenter.